moonstone

The plot considered
first in the mind –
wraps a prince
in a beggar's cloak.

A down cast act,
with talons drawn
wrapped in tattered shreds.
Outwit outfit,
friend of Athena.
Test deception
with deception.

In the mind,
artisan designs
architectural maze.
He lies in bed,
envisioning
complicated corners,
a grid more complex
than riddles.

Sees it
to seize it's
wild snare
and confound it there
thrashing in echoes.

In a mathematician's mind,
aortic stem
and arctic poles
with calculus,
combine a force field
of human
electric pulse.

Numbered sequences
magnetize
the spherical ship.
Envelope and
execute the sketch-
catching wind to sail
a heart's adventure.

In the mind,
silence is
an attentive muse.
Quiet there
and chaos here,
a loom of ideas
infuse
the evening thought
with a sailor's knot.

In the journey,
the gift of moonstone,
as sacred as players
bent by their lines,
like Hermes message
over wine.

The stone guides
home to find
attentive protective warmth
of another star.

Careful, careful
a stormy gale
may swallow life.
Artisan considers course
and with integrity
under dark force
leaves a word.

Abide
in a better glow,
stone
lucky as the moon
you know.

All of life,
the heart affords
is first considered
in the mind.

eclipse

Does one pay more attention when life begins
than in the coasting, tween, adult, mid-life scenes,
abruptly re-focusing in the end?

What does payment of attention mean?

Do we fade like static snow;
an eclipse of moments?

Chapter one: *light interrupts womb.*
Drift -drift- drift.
Final chapter: *reentry into unknown.*

New little humans
fist-y punches,
observant, exposed.
They sleep, they squeal and squeak
in bright enormity.

Swaddle me.
I was fine the way you found me.

And elderly,
the slow turning down
of sound and sight
prepare for goodnight.
Brevity
eclipses the *in between.*

It passed so fast,
I passed so fast
from light to fog to darkening.

veil

The veil
to face transcendent age
when bleak is clear,
and fear is myth
in an isolated cage.

Theories are veiled,
hidden truths of youth,
sweet like china bells.
Psychoanalyze or hypothesize
conditional human wishing.

Our skin,
argumentatively thin,
and this selfless coursework
begins again.

Veil of incarnation,
of pretty, petty decency,
entwined in
unveiled clarity.

I could say what I want but humanity incriminates me.
The bride is tame, supposedly.

The veil of grooms
(I heard them
in my brother's room)
patchwork hope
and terrified bone.
Mommy's kiss and red light's bliss.

A light, arid mask.
Pungent, pulsing sacrament.

The veil was temple torn.
We expected cloth so thick
to withstand.
But it ripped
floor to pitch
as the choir began.

Unveiling union of vow and veil –
wing to fly or wind to sail
between the pages
a plot change,
an identity exchange.

Love stands in plentitude
with a train.
in this ancestral line
we kick and scream
to untie,
then rest
in ties that bind.

fire

Fire is
winter's wool throw
for the chill sway
blue blaze tango
in a birded wood world.

Hypnotic chemical bond
adheres to strength
in combustion.
Oxygenated
flashing wand.
Root systems conjoin
in seasonal sleep.

Ice dies,
desire for fires rise.
Soft gray ash
of oaken willow
weeps.

Coupled with an
inevitable scene.
Chemical extraction in verse,
smoldering.

eden ash

Now that Eden smolders,
(the price of emission,
the cost of omission,
shady decision,
evil intention,
past blasphemous
riotous animals)
we shuffle out
slump-shouldered
through pickled leaves.

Limping hedgehogs.
Bluefaced shrugs.
Desolate harvest baskets.

I look to him,
he looks to her,
she looks to them.
We all look drugged.

Shreds of Hiroshima's dress,
sweaty palms of dolls
shoveled in piles,
trapped without windows.

Death comes sure
when temptation
trumps consideration,
drooling over
dragon-guarded gold.

Now Eden smolders
and our grandchildren
with metal shoes
will pop exhaust bubbles.

Go to your bed,
seal up your tombs.
Eden's ash is
no prophetic tune.

Around supper tables,
schoolchildren waste epiphanies
on distracted populations.
Warn fat-faced, sopping
hedge fund bastards
in eloquent elementary verbiage.

Power mutes
voice of low repute.
Lend her thine ear-
with a sharp point,
erase the bottom line.
Retrace
the verdant fruit laden vine
for them
before apple infection
makes masters of war
look like all men.

tombs

The man of the tombs in the Gerasene
naked, cutting, tortured with voices
was local entertainment.

Attentive healer named him *'our wounded boy.'*

With surgical precision,
cognitive scalpel,
he sent the boy's demons
into a herd of suicidal pigs.

He was discharged with new clothes and peace treaties.

White with terror,
the crowd ran the doctor out of town
like two thousand doomed swine.

Accusers were more terrified of the healer
than the demons.
*Gavels and feed troughs
are sold on the same aisle.*

hunger

If Solomon tipped my chin
quoting wisdom and his song,
fleece or moonlight,
would it end?

If, in English moors,
draped over winter's field
the first green flash of gold, or
in the recitation
of dizzy shepherd affection
could it end?

If offered the loyalty
of courtly love-
Lancelot's allegiance,
if Camelot were my garden-
would the heart have enough?
Isn't loneliness cruel?

What *if* I had a potion-
if every thought precipitated
an appearance,
a bone clad phantom or
a resuscitated ghost?

Or, if home were void
of task and triviality,
if whispering returned-
would the mind
stop its incessant
suggestion that I exist alone?

I asked my father this morning for help.
My battery sparking in a dark cave
trapped in exhaustion with self.

His cherry-faced joy
cooed,
not with anticipated scolding,
but cheered me in the furrow.

Yes, you are on a quest,
embedded maps of paradise
flash like the portrait of a blink.
More of love, yes,
stay desperate for more.

The evidence your sight is clear
and mud forsakes you in this.
The feast, and wedding fleece
awaits at the end
of solemn roads.

bridge of sighs

Kneel beside the hearth and wait
steep wine and press a linen cape
tend herb and plants for soup, in case
he comes for you, mid-autumn tide
forsake the cursed' bridge of sighs.

There was another lover's isle
where wings of wax melted the son.
Imprisoned joy - *a vanished boy*
feathers wash up on the shore
floating by the bridge of sighs.

The daughter of the sun, alone
King David's lion, warm beside.
Jewels of Jove laid row by row,
father's gift and curse of woe.
All are borrowed lovers, though.
She feels her wings melt off and flow
below the icy bridge of sighs.

Is it a spirit pressing deep?
Knocks night by night upon her dream
breathless, fevered, heaving close.
Cheeks flush with a bourbon glow,
but wakes in hellish undertow.

Teach the heart a patient pace
and plant the spilling vines in place
along the bridge of longing, sighs.

Craft mends fast a ravaged heart
a careful stitch, of song and art.
Gold breath of God, attentive eyes.
Innocent and in order set.
Holy love, eternal, yet
time and breath will be goodbye.
Meet by the bridge of sighs and fly.

horizon

Does the sky tire
and rest on the ocean?
Does the sea rise
and reach for the sky?
In that face-to-face
place of their meeting,
horizon unveils her surprise.

Romance is a wind for the water,
and water, the wells of the air.
The sky gives
and rests on her rocking.
The sea reaches up, pulls him near.

The starfish then pulse into being.
The seahorse twins mirror star steed.
The flying fish caught on a star wire,
conceived love of sky and his sea.

spirit and flesh

On either side, a prison visit
divided by a thin sheet of glass.

Byzantine throne, Roman bathhouse.
So thin, hands reach through
and grab handfuls of salt
or disrobe in a king's court to bathe.

In case files,
the spirit calms,
the flesh suggests.
In all cases,
palms of healing press,
but palms of longing press back.
Friday palm branch dress or Easter nakedness?

Spirit, flesh
stare the other down
and hold their hollow ground.
It's a drag~
pleas and pleaaseee.
Steel equipment,
legions of soldiers and years of tension.

Internal platoon
standing on a pelvic womb
and the officers beat on the glass.
Visit's over.

But the delicious morning
births a destructive mourning.
Red lips, crown of thorns.

siren tone

Ithaca
with her bolted bed
and virtuous thread
is half magnetic
as the unknown.

If given choice
to sail or weave
knowing how fragile
the glass of sea,
I'd run aboard
ten years or so
to conquer myself.

You could go.
The most adept
with Cyclops spear,
fire tender,
wit and wise storyteller
map-reader, mind reader
to attend storm demon
while I dream.

Dreamland is unhinged
from court and gravity.
Science, art and history
meet at the edge of perception
browsing coastlines to find
Circe collections
for the return.

Then, ghostlike dives
from greatest height
to darkest depth:
heaven ceiling-
supine masterpiece

and the *gut punch plummet*
to hellish tile
of underworld snow.

Can one hear their own siren song –
honeyed pitch
or is it behind cognition
in the womb of a dream region?

Is the song ethereal
rehearsal of Eve's daughter?
"*Come near*, the song trills.
Closer, the black abyss."

Hush it, quiet it,
wail it out into deep midnight.
The drape of dreams
is a poet's seam.
Isn't hunger innate?

As Ithaca becomes
a freckle in thine eye
the fierce biting undertow pulls.

Cinnamon hall, lovers' walls
warlords tamed with words.

Counsel, see the guards.
Feet bound in gold
with Helios breath,
the mast woven
into a warm white dress.

Paradise lost, a divine comedy
A comedy of errors
As I dream in a midsummer's night.

Awake, I find a true desert,
smooth sober horizon
in the dead center of Ithaca.

40 days of hunger and vision
with no human immunity-
where when temptation
is conquered and ends,
the buffet of angel food begins.

hymn of neptune

Golden rod, on stage resounds
a triune storied love.

The ancient score,
our bloodline
in dust formed
broken bone.

Audience of livestock
orchestral center row.
Barn wood floor,
oil lamp-lit
earth's cello,
heaven's bow.

The trumpet's
breathing black hole
a meteor's
train of wings
Astronomer lens exposing
the son, omniscient king.

Apprentice
perspective
summation.
The wise men
silenced by babe,
whose faith in stars,
the plot lines,
compass gold
and myrrh parade.

Rhetorical radiant bard
prophet bent
in eloquent woe

A throne
of splintered crossbeam
a night of holy prose.

Mother bleeding, breaking.
Her womb, a covenant arc.
The players bow, embracing
the hymn of Neptune starts.

salt

Salt ruins.
Her sideways glance
shaped Lot's new memorial:
preservative defiance.
Statuesque, seasonal dress.
The apple, salty too.

Savory flavor behavior
aspirate fruit's juice
yet renders water fatal.
Not a drop.

Perfect crust
earth shell,
temperatures of hell.

Salt-packed wounds are
primal scream extractions.
A quench of infection
with a healing sting.

Prism prison
voluntary dome
schooner skirt,
skin of sun
NaCl assembly line
sodium, breath, chloride.

Abundance crafts a panic room.
Abstinence, a seizure catalyst.

Drip or shaker,
salt of the earth.
No preservative.

toolshed

The telescope
is a tool
for razored erasure
of distance
here to the celestial sphere.

A yard of
light year
is torn for
Orion.
Seam rip and fabric fray.
Scissored precision,
snip milky space away.

The sandblast tool
smooths a bull nose curvature.
He snorts the meteor spray.

Silver truth tool-
arrow and rule
shedding whip,
hoisted hip- slip knot-
word by word
fire branded.

Master tool
cuts stone shame to sand.
Mason chisels ethos-
hammered marble shape
till mouth agape,
thigh bone
polished ache
swallowed jewel
in Hades gait.

parlor

The celestial parlor
-that which consumes daydream-
has coordinates:
latitude, longitude, aptitude.

Ten light-years
of sailor's navigation
plot and course
by midnight sun.

The dark earth
heaven's sounding weight
Where mortal men and Endymion
stretches arms
to ride with Selene
towards a stars'
worth of dreams.

The mortal man
stirs her immortal plan.
Finite parlor,
plush fragrant
deep warmth
fleeting.
Yet still
she steers the steed
with increased intensity
to push
through lightyear seas
towards a mortal heart
for that brief heat,
to leave him beaming
in infinite sleep.

rapids

Rapids gulp inverted breath,
swish round her rocky jaws.
Ruckus of frenzied mossy teeth
scream snort of wild swine calls.

Rapids are hurried, rapidly
suctioned like swimmer lungs.
Crushing blend of biting bits
from old adventurous bone.

Drunken submarine cauldron
smash happenstance to sand.
Buried under boulder,
waterlog dead shoe man.

Stay afloat, whatever it costs you
for your blue and bloodshot eyes.
The reefer ticket salesman
snickers when you lose your sight.

Tenderizing torture tendrils
throw stick man in sick cycle ride.
Limb stab your eye, death on her mind
a blender of foam cyanide.

But oh, the thrill, is never gone.
Ride me on and on and on.
Wide-eyed thrill in white water pit,
where the rapids dip,
where the tension grips.

The gulping plunge pulls heavy
river's muscle a grip of stone.
The guide stirs paddle battered
steps on her gritty foam.

How thrilling the motion passion
swirled speed in fixated wind.
Curl toes and ride on sun-ward.
Still waters rise round the bend.

profile

The unknown
serves a poet food,
an appetite for awe.

The stone girl's profile
peers from an Arizona ridge.

She isn't prostrate.
Too dumbfounded to worship,
glazed in baked stupor.

Tree bone submerse,
immersed
chiseled.
Peaches and mandarin
fill in cheekbone.
Lips pursed patient
for lips of the wind.

Press your ear
to the canyon wall,
warm as Sunday bread.
Cupped close -
lobe skin to stone,
just a minute or two
like a daughter listening
to waves
recorded
in a conch shell.

Do you hear the gallop
of a cave drawn stag
chipping jabs like ancient
pounding grounded hooves?

Unknown in origin,
unknown in tone,
unknown form.
Ear to the earth's vibration –
the fire is coming
the fire is coming.

For thunderstorm,
the red clay drum,
bird and horse
in a restless anxious flutter.
The girl stretched
her body out
across the desert
to mute
its old secret.

seven swans, seven deadly sins, seven curses, seven
    wonders

quiet, all,
he steps into the glow.

imprint

A photographer's lens
borrows light.
Focused framed moments.
Photography catches poetry.

Poetry is the
art of wording.
The articulation of
imprinted images.

A painter first peers,
then flips introspection-
teaching hands the transfer
of imagination to canvas.

Music is the
sound love makes,
the layers of life beneath sight.
Spirit's soundtrack.

The curious
ignore consequence.
Wisdom waits
with reverent caution.
Scientist, sage.

Happiness pays well.
Oui, love.
How lovely the image,
how soothing the notion,
how magnetic
the consideration.

Father, artist, musician, lover, poet, beautiful, light
    engineer's imprint.

More beautiful still
when one
once hypnotized
wakes with hope.
A glimpse of dreamlike
eternal love,
visible with internal lens,
to hush fear
and live
verdant
as an apple tree.

hold

To hold someone
in a sleep
slows the hurried world.

The care not to stir them
a sweet marveling
lifts eyes
to what
you hurried by.

Clear focus
dial to the wren outside,
her proud chest.
Puff whistle pipe.

All that busy-ness blinds,
stopping to hold
spotlights fragile,
silent tinsel.
Woodpecker,
fourth note deep
oblivious his sound
pounds
hammer
to wood
of coral bells.

But the baby wakes and wants down.

If you hold my attention,
I give it like a tithe,
you see.
Ten percent.
The other ninety,
fantastically spent.

Wise ones learn
hold,
never be captive,
but captivate.
Hold steady,
hold your tongue,
eyes of wisdom
hold me.

hen

The feather dust hen
paces and pecks
at her pie in the sky,
crimping crust with forked feet.

Knuckles of bough bone
a slight of hand, mind you,
entitled "morning and evening, one ordinary day"
in illegible chicken scratch.

In the rich candied landscape
of deciduous delicacies
his hardware store hen
clucks content as an Imperial child.

Philosophers prescribe:

"walk in simplicity, twenty–five miles or so, for proper
        contented rest by close of day."
As effective as holding or being held,
my experimental philosophies convey.

A thrill-oil teems under wing
she snuffs the henhouse.
Ignores the dangerous could be wolves,
and at dusk, burrows in a roost
gargling into a fermented coo.

He could reach and eased her down for me.
His own wingspan,
broad expansive hands
know the coaxing of her grip.

I settle and let her nest in my arms,
exquisitely dressed in a nightgown
of blush eyelash ruching.

Rooting in the bend-
I am her limb.
In the wood
where fire reigns,
the thrill of warm
fragile care
is like the ascent
into a split oak.

Fragile enough to die,
or brave enough
on chilly tips of October
to hide my bones
in the crook of your limbs.

friend

When my eyes fall closed-
soft like the bow
under a mother's wing-
a warm glow washes over
the rest of me.

Tension, angst and indecision
release into a womb pose--
quiet, still, belonging.

I listen to the tone
in your storied voice.
I record honesty and insecurity.
I listen to you laugh
and harmonize.

Instinctive memory
like prehistoric fossilized vision -
in a tomb-like, marbled gallery
white wool felted scar zippers.

Art is the highest wealth.

We view ice as isinglass,
the cold as fire tender,
slosh beyond
the present mud.

And if your twin is gone-
if she couldn't stay
if the coil was unwound-
then it was to gift me
with company,
a cord within reach
to lasso a bird's
ribbon of words
with this song.

dessert menu

Sweet undressed rows of sugar cane
needles quiver threading the record's groove
Tiptoes on a wooden parlor floor
The baker's apron and nutmeg spoons
Nap in a hammock in Eve's leaves
innumerable flower gardens of sturdy stalk
love's intoxication, the first finger weaving
Cracked ooze of crème brule
Cotton sheets dry on a southern clothesline
Silk hair corn dolls
Candlelit smile
A quiet canopy of Savannah trees
A pair of heavy robes in a borrowed room
Window covering pulled open
Oak fire with birch curls
Rain drumming on a tin
oil painting and finger skating
bourbon ice and citrus slice
a hidden nest of peregrines
beard of Dickens' gentleman
ruddy-faced shepherd boy
Solomon's mother's rooftop view
sweet feed calf, Milan's Duomo birds
Clockmaker in my father's Germany
Mary's holy stable inn, Augustine's confession
Venice mime, violinist on the stair
jazz piano bar, hands smoothing my hair
black mountain, blue moon, browns canyon
Yellowstone, Greenland, Red River valley
Anticipation.

dinner date

A dinner dress:
Pink melon slip
thin tissue silk
lemon tint lace
doll and her date.

Dinner dressing:
slow roast boil
carcass and coal
chanting, enchanted
wild boar brine
brandy blood wine.

To dress for dinner:
bathe your ache
it's time
to wash your soul
in cedar and lime.

You are hungry, I know
it will always be so.

In the fire basin,
copper pot cage
garlic bangles
and butter shoes
root flesh and juice
chef embraces
sous chef's
interpretation
truffle shavings
snow over
shoulder blades.

Stems are trimmed.
Velvet petals blush

in table scape vase
off-set the glow
of her eyes
looking for yours.

Delicate speak
placates wait.
Gentleman,
cocktail bait.

Kitchen steam
blanche and braise.
Quenching deglazes
oil spoon and swirl.
Roast and broil,
ladle soup,
dressing plates
to service tray
for lime sorbet.

Walk to take
a tabled place.
The chef, the guest,
dressing, dressed.

Noting how the face
across the storied
plate satiates
hunger more
than dinner course
cascade.

I love most an
end satiation.
Serving fills more
than if he
filled my cup
with a thimble of port.

The heart,
most hungry vessel,
if satisfied,
calls the rest dessert.
If starving,
even a feast will not serve.

indigo

Between the waking worlds I row
hook eye lines, collecting prose.
It's deep, and vision overflows
immersed, I swim in indigo.

I took your hand, I love it so.
Stained glass hour of dusk arose.
Then violet sang the blues we know.
Crooning, the world glowed indigo.

Linden wood in light brush stroke.
The hour of a cherry snow.
Guests with gifts, of painted hope.
Jewels frame the centered indigo.

You, the hue of ocean cave,
illumination great white sheen.
Forlorn storm, a whaler's wave
or ink well full of granular scenes.

I've sewn all the layers round.
Day dress dyed in a deeper glow.
Crafted, sculpted, color drenched.
All delicious indigo.

color

Is brandy or whiskey
the color unsure?
Battle shot stiff,
pour just one more.
Heart break erasure,
famous for shame.
Paper ship sinks
in Crown Royal flame.

Fire liquid light drip
in white sip sunrise.
Too close to my mind,
guide whispering wise.
Riddle or rhyme,
sleight of hand,
down the pipe.
Intrigue over ice,
in a diamond white light.

Rust fades to melon,
it mellows your spine.
Hypnotic smoke stoning
in high noon shine.
Heart pulsating clear.
The blockade's refined.
Saint's ennobling will,
a high bar to climb.

If yellow is heat,
limoncello flames.
If blue is free,
101 highways tamed.
If red is love,
it bleeds deep port seas.
Green screams her gale-
Irish whiskey,

side of freeze.

Mix oracle notes,
braid hue blended slow.

Entwining like twins,
sleep sweet toe to toe.

A plumb wine barrel
for bathing between.
A colorless,
senseless,
concessional scene.

peach

I absent-heartedly swallow
an island or star shell.
Inside, insular force field adrift,
drawn to fire on a matchbook raft.

Just one deep peek into a wishing whale.

When my lips part, agape
like sweet echoic memory,
serenity turns a face
soft as a peach.

Why, I'd quite forgotten
what potency there'd be,
thriving in intimacy
and stirred in currents.

Fervent spread
of prolific vines,
the vast periscope
it entwines,
sandman's wink,
the crystal brine.

See the way
flesh of a summer peach
underneath fuzzy skin satisfies,
like a long flat breeze
will seize your sweating.

The pit slips in
Just a moment
in your cheek.
No! Not ready to release.
The brevity
before you can think,

the dust covered
summer thirst,
quenched
and the pit left empty
as you sync again
with the air.

Like the way
you stay out alone,
late in wrinkled bedclothes
to gaze on a strawberry moon.
Barefoot, behind the pain
swaying alone to a tune.
Hum and owling,
elated and late.
To howl her soundwave
as a volt of starlight
jumpstarts
a darkened place you hate.
And reveals, like a flash,
The silhouetted vision
of an island inside.

Moon sand,
supple peaches
till the ladder falls
and your feet swing
and dip through brit
from bow and stern.

And left for tomorrow
one last catch –
humming in the mast song
of the swallow brit and brine
Island sand, peach moonshine.

scent

Love, while you exhale
I inhale your heart breathing
it sweetens life's dream
your scent is like sun.
Lifeline breeze
and clean like heat.
Joy inhalation
lavender and clove.
Cinnamon smoke
so fragrant.
The kiss of dewdrop
when we hug goodbye.
It's in the curve
of your neck
soul scent memory.

heron

Southern marsh,
fenced in cattails,
is governed
by the boa and bodice
of a blue heron
whose debutante posture
defies the mud batter glue
on her sticky shoes.

Mosquitoes' prey and snip
like neon
zip signs
soon as you turn to sin
live oaks host ghosts
in a haunted historical wind.

Spanish moss itches
And unrest
is under the rest
of our somatic symptoms.
One hundred years,
cholera,
longing
eco-blue
aligned malaise.

You cannot dive or die
heron bird.
The creek is shallow
as a weather word.
Nothing breathes
that easy leaves.

Solitude isolates
then inhales
another disease.

Viral as torpedo heat.
Neither equator nor pole
begin or end
the circled world.
And without flight
we would rather freeze.

It's cold to know,
it burns to believe.
Assuredness,
ginger as heron feet.
Infinite as these moments feel.
Deceptive and fleeting
as a southern marsh breeze.

amelia

*"I cannot guarantee to endure at all times the confinements of even an
attractive cage."* AME

In aviation, Amelia,
propeller blades shave
gravity's old face.

What better fills the cockpit's
warm humming purr?
Locked in,
con-swooned to fuse cords
of vision's placenta,
tangled
in climax and catapult.
The cathartic branding
of birth certified pilot wing.

A girl can crook her legs
and shepherd a wild scene
of low-hanging limbs
adjusting dials till speed
pushes wheels into the belly
of a yellow canary.
A snappy leathered cap-sized cage.

The grave, breath trades
for ever-clean air.

What a brief gift,
that gilded age
a bee's intensity,
a bird's ease
obeying the
wild in thee.

Amelia, *was it a nosedive fade?*
A figure-eight exit stage wave?
A swimmingly perfect
aeronautical dial ringing space?
Did your spine never dip or seep
in the sea to bathe?

And then it seems~
Like light pops
she melts into
Maestro's bluesy tune
in pilot skin,
propeller pinwheel then
ta-da
pigeons replaced with vaporous grace.

Correspondence will wait for him
cross the silky milk stream
staring off into her secret dream.

Amelia, when I write to you,
I ask if Saint-Exupery
had French wine
Bordeaux and Brie,
a top hat or leather pilot's cap,
chocolate pinwheels on a wand
stories of a pilot plot.
The philosophical wind
a mind cannot untie
to unpack
a knapsack
and jump.

The aviator poets,
evaporate into thin bliss
And let the letters,
the urgent mail
rain like snow below

runway runaways
close as ghosts.

"a sky as pure as water bathed the stars and brought them out" ASE

*"the stars seemed near enough to touch and never before have I seen
so many" AME*

frozen jazz

Murano glass tour
crashed sad, but the
sound, pitched perfect
rat-a-tat-tat tune
like Poe's swanky cat bird.

It was pushed, he said.
It swang
like a swing dance dive, man
then burst
into hard ache
screamin' like a
cymbal flash,
bits and splinters lashed.

What a sick drumstick hit,
just like that.
Turquoise eyeglass
rush to the bleed
like a savior to
fade the stage lights on
incomplete jazz.

Wanna watch that shipwreck sink, mate?
A little front-page news?
Titanical confusion.
Haywire, live wire
gravitational blues.

Think of all that
bass line score.
All the high-hat encore.

All the jazz froze
when mourning
hit it hard.

She pulled the strings,
tied the pieces
to a
bathtub ring.
Paper-thin undertaker man
Soot eye chimney sweep band
swept up tuba tracks,
mopped waves to the can.

Last call, SOS address,
elbow grease and
close up.

Throw a rope.
The tour is done.
The jazz all froze
when the tile explodes.

violin

The airy craft of a violin
is curved to sound
like a king's curls.

The violinist arcs
then tilts her chin
as if to watch ducklings pass
over the bridge.

Still, feigning sleep,
in a shadow box of spotlight
appears the shape
of a dream doll and her violin.

Holding the bow,
arrowed in thread
she shakes her wrists,
thrashing out shapes
of hallowed notes
from her chest
like butterflied confetti.

We barely survive such surprise.

*The concerto draws the darling's love for her bird on the
    drapery above the orchestral pit, and the swooping call
    of his wings beat against the wind of the bow rushing
    over the belly of the violin's cave.*

The Lark Ascending.
How soft
euphoria fades
when bow and violin
rest at her waist
and in silence
startled, she wakes.

labor

Labor halts and calls
an inexperienced stagecoach,
in a flushed blush,
breathtaking gallop and woe.

Steering, jeering
cross the timeline
past ancient clay cultures.
Dignity hangs
from a branch,
enduring each
instinctive spur.

The usurping labor
squeezes the swollen abdomen
like wringing a soaking dish rag,
twisting tight as a vice until
every tension is sensed.

She flips, stretches her heel
like a bootstrap
in the rib cage cell.
Ya! Ya!
Hushed beeps *echo echo echo*
until unnatural silver appears
and folded in fear
teaches mother to pray.
Silent night, Holy night
The baby crowned
in velvet down,
accolade of divinity.

ride home

Last evening,
I lifted my dancer
home over autumn fields.

Her pirouette and fouette
grazed a tempered sunset.
Wind-blown acres of stage,
stags and doves
on horizon's line.

Amber and wheat plowed brown
eaten by a silver columbine.
The profuse perfumed earth,
deep-breath smell of dusky dust
arrested she and me
mid-harmony
and we locked eyes.

One cannot gasp
with enough depth
-even landscape sized breaths-
when fields are harvest-stirred.

The glittered litter
catches fire-light finale.

Smoking bales
lassoed with twine
surrender to November.
But my dancer, here,
in her pink tights,
leotard and pursed lips,
her sharp jawline and lilac eyes,
holds my hand
for landing.

She spied the orange fire first,
a mandarin orange blaze
gypsy mandolin tune
fiddling in the shadow
and we pulled over to watch the nest twigs
hug goodbye to one another.

But evening is just the beginning.
She will dance through
the land of sweets until dawn.
I, with the violin swan,
sail and strum
hand in hand
patient as a
spring dream
in winter's buried land.

red hot pokers

My mother announced
as we escaped this morning
she'd stolen more
Red-hot pokers
and had some for me.
She knows I love every flower I meet
and steals them from
abandoned homesteads she knew.
Old heirloom beauty.
It's my inheritance.

I tuck them in with earthworms,
those hibernating roots.
Aiding and a bedding
with my mother, shotgun rider.

She sang along
to her favorite Arlo Guthrie song.
"Good morning, America how are ya?
Don't cha know me, I'm your native son?
I'm the train they call the city of New Orleans.
I'll be gone 500 miles when the day is done."

And the October sun
 the dizzy caffeine
felt like we'd been healed.

I took her home
she watched me and pop
load the red-hot pokers.
Shifty box full with dirt spillin.
He slammed the trunk rough and gritty.
She waved and pointed
to her own red-hot pokers
 "there they are."

Little fires everywhere she goes.

I watched them
weave arms
like one wild vine
as she pulled her leg along.
Bonnie and Clyde,
then turned the volume up
for our favorite song
Morning Has Broken
and coasted down the drive.

still life

This bowerbird nest I rest in:
one vintage green postal box,
two emerald sages,
three lime peacocks on tinsel ivy
all hang
in *still life* pose.

But not always *so.*
Once fluttered with immediacy
eggshells, seashells, rattles and rails.

When chirping ended,
the kaleidoscope shows and
crowning prances,
a thousand little seed feasts
to tip a nestled chorus,
transformed into an
emotional fall
with no prophetic wings.

The birds just bloomed.

Green breathtaking bowered years,
a towerful of flapping.
Out on a limb,
strands and strings
of heels and hairpins,
silver stitches, coq au vin
like the wild tearing tease
of a wrapping paper.

But tide pools swirl,
the young bird's gaze adrift
on the cocktail bay.
Bower boys strut,
orange and gray,

a new collection,
stronger limbs
arrange trinkets
in woodland hay.

When the bower nest emptied,
sunset led me to another.
I exhaled long and low
with shiny eyes
like my mother,
while those grand strand birds,
warble throated culture
hum dirges and morph
into *still life*.

Once space is shared,
don't fear the end
of a bowerbird show.
But consider the price
of a nest that's cold.
Lost dreams alone
will make you old.

about atmosphere press

Atmosphere Press is an independent, full-service publisher for excellent books in all genres and for all audiences. Learn more about what we do at atmospherepress.com.

We encourage you to check out some of Atmosphere's latest releases, which are available at Amazon.com and via order from your local bookstore:

I Would Tell You a Secret, poetry by Hayden Dansky

Aegis of Waves, poetry by Elder Gideon

Streetscapes, poetry by Martin Jon Porter

Feast, poetry by Alexandra Antonopoulos

River, Run! poetry by Caitlin Jackson

Poems for the Asylum, poetry by Daniel J. Lutz

Licorice, poetry by Liz Bruno

Etching the Ghost, poetry by Cathleen Cohen

Spindrift, poetry by Laurence W. Thomas

A Glorious Poetic Rage, poetry by Elmo Shade

Numbered Like the Psalms, poetry by Catharine Phillips

Verses of Drought, poetry by Gregory Broadbent

Canine in the Promised Land, poetry by Philip J. Kowalski

PushBack, poetry by Richard L. Rose

Modern Constellations, poetry by Kendall Nichols

Whirl Away Girl, poetry by Tricia Johnson

about the author

Nicole Verrone wrote *Nest of Stars* over six months, after a twenty-year hiatus to raise four daughters. Born in North Carolina, she spent summers on her grandparents' dairy farm where the poetry of an uncle lost in a tragic car accident was on display. This formative event instilled the beauty and brevity of life through verse. A writer since adolescence, her first poem was published in the local newspaper in 1986. She earned a BA in English from UNC-Greensboro, taught high school literature, and currently serves on an educational team as accreditation and continuing education consultant in the healthcare industry.

Verrone lives vicariously through the accounts of adult daughters studying to become healthcare professionals and providers. Her youngest, a pre-teen, still hangs out in the nest. Verrone has been married a long time to a flyfishing guru and her best pal. She attempts to embrace intangible gifts, fill time and space with art and music, reading and philosophy, and has an unquenchable thirst for stories and travel.

Nest of Stars is her first published work. Cover art was gifted by her dear friend and favorite dinner guest, Sarah Helser.